# Traditional Tales
# of the World

Happy House

# About Wise & Wide

- A systematic 6-level English reading program based on Lexile® measures
- Diverse and interesting topics chosen from the elementary curriculums of Korea and English speaking western countries
- Well-written books in various forms including fiction stories, descriptive texts, and classics retold
- The informative but original fiction stories grab your interest, leading to the easy and clear understanding of the educational content.
- Improve thinking skills with solid after-reading activities at all levels of the series.

**Wise & Wide** is a 6-level English reading program that consists of 60 books and each level is systematically divided by Lexile® measures. The Lexile® Framework for Reading is the most popular reading measuring system in American formal education curriculums and many English programs. Over 20 out of 50 states in the U.S. mark Lexile® measures directly on students' final report cards and over 300 well-known publishers adopt and use Lexile® measures.

Experience many kinds of readings written by professional writers from the U.S. and England. They used interesting topics that were carefully chosen after analyzing elementary curriculums from around the world including Korea, the U.S., England, and Australia among many others. Comprehensive after-reading activities including graphic organizers, speaking tasks, and After-reading Tests are ready for you.

## Levels in the series and their corresponding Lexile® measures

| Level | Lexile® measures | U.S. Grade |
| --- | --- | --- |
| Level 1 | Below 200L | Pre K - K |
| Level 2 | 190L - 400L | Lower Grade 1 |
| Level 3 | 350L - 530L | Upper Grade 1 |
| Level 4 | 420L - 650L | Grade 2 |
| Level 5 | 520L - 940L | Grade 3 - 4 |
| Level 6 | 830L - 1070L | Grade 5 - 6 |

* Smart Readers: Wise & Wide level 1 is applicable to the preschool level in the U.S.
* The source of the relationship between Lexile® measures and U.S. school grades: CCSS(Common Core State Standards) FOR ENGLISH LANGUAGE ARTS, APPENDIX A (2012, which is used by 45 states in the U.S.)

# Topic List

| | Level 1 | Level 2 | Level 3 | Level 4 | Level 5 | Level 6 |
|---|---|---|---|---|---|---|
| Book 1 | Science>Biology: The hibernation of animals Story | Science>Biology: Living and nonliving things Story | Science>Biology> Animals & the Environment: Sea otters Story | Environment> Living with nature: The diver & the persimmon tree Story | Science>Biology> Animal: Amazing animals of the Amazon Story | Science>Biology: Germs, transmitted diseases Story |
| Book 2 | Literature> World classics: Aesop's fables Story | Literature> Traditional fairy tale: Old tales about stones Story | Social Studies> Economy: To run a business to make and save money Story | Science>Biology> Plants: Photosynthesis Story | Science>Earth science: Earth's layers, earthquakes, volcanoes, and earth's atmosphere Report | Mathematics> Sequence: The golden ratio & the Fibonacci sequence Story |
| Book 3 | Science>Physics: How shadows are formed Story | Literature> World classics: Peter Pan Story | Science>Scientific technology: Nanobots Story | Literature>Myths: World's creation stories Story | Literature> Legend: The story of King Arthur Story | Literature>Myths: Constellation myths Story |
| Book 4 | Literature> Traditional literature: The Talmud Story | Science>Biology> Animal: Polar bears Story | Science>Biology> Animal: Mountain gorillas Story | Social Studies> Cultural anthropology: Amazing ancient cultures of the world Story | Science> Earth science: Clouds and weather Story | Literature> Human & animals: The friendship between a girl and a horse Story |
| Book 5 | Social Studies> Ethics: Rules in daily life Story | Science>Biology: The five senses Report | Social Studies> Cultural anthropology: Astonishing festivals Report | Art>Music: Stories from two operas Story | Social Studies> World culture & history: The Renaissance Story | Sports> Board sports: Surfing & snowboarding Story |
| Book 6 | Social Studies> World geography & travel: Tourist attractions around the world Story | Science>Biology> Animal: Dinosaurs Story | Science> Astronomy: The solar system Story | Social Studies> People: Three great people who overcame hardships Story | Science>Scientific technology: The wonderful world of robots Report | Art>Music: Composers of the Romantic Era Report |
| Book 7 | Science> Space science: The life of astronauts Report | Social Studies> Cultural anthropology: Mythological monsters from around the world Report | Mathematics> Elementary mathematics: Numbers, measurement, shapes and data Report | Science & Social Studies> Technology & culture: Inventions from around the world Report | Art>Works of art: Famous paintings Report | Social Studies> Human & animals: Animals in action for human Report |
| Book 8 | Social Studies> Cultural anthropology: Various living cultures of the world Story | Art>Music: Instruments in the orchestra Story | Social Studies> Life safety: Learning and using outdoor survival skills Story | Social Studies> History: The California Gold Rush Report | Social Studies & Science> Psychology: Psychology in everyday life Story | Literature> World classics: The Merchant of Venice Story |
| Book 9 | Social Studies> Jobs: Interviews about jobs Report | Science>Scientific technology: Developments in technology in different times Story | Social Studies> Politics>Election: Running for 3rd grade class president Story | Literature> World classics: Stories of Sherlock Holmes Story | Literature> World classics: Adrift in the Pacific Story | Social Studies> History & People: Great world leaders in history Report |
| Book 10 | Literature>Traditional fairy tale: Eastern and Western folk tales on the same theme Story | Sports>Winter sports: Various aspects of some Winter Olympic sports Report | Literature> World classics: Short stories by O. Henry Story | Sports> Ball games: Various aspects of popular ball games Report | Social Studies> History: Famous events that changed world history Report | Art & Social Studies> Art: Stories about the creation, distribution, and preservation of paintings Report |

10 books in each level will be published.

# How to Use This Book

## • Before Reading

You can easily find the topic and what kind of story you are about to read.

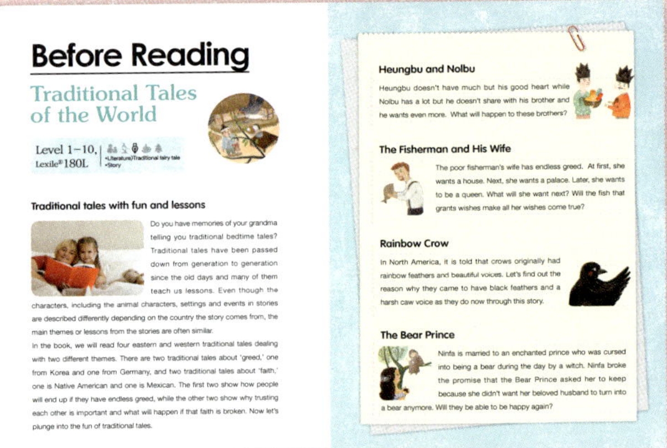

## • The text

All the stories were written by professional writers from the U.S. and England, so you will read authentic and appropriate English sentences and expressions in every book in the series.

## • Pop Quiz

Check out right away if you understand what you have just read by solving a pop quiz that checks your comprehension.

## • Key Words

The key words and expressions on each page are listed for you to easily study them.

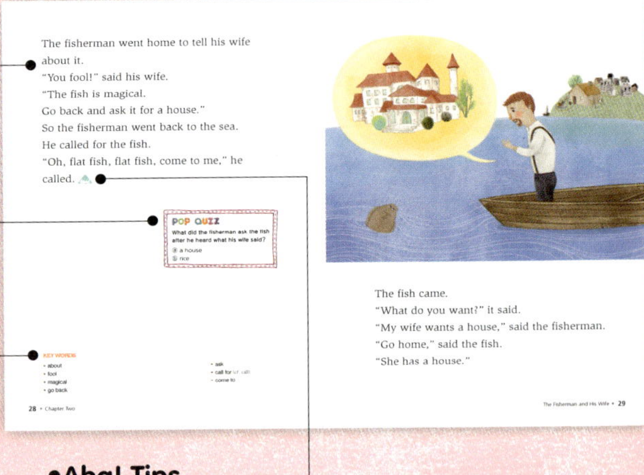

## • Aha! Tips

Download free Korean explanations at *www.ihappyhouse.co.kr* for all of the sentences marked with "Aha!". These explain cultural, scientific, and economic knowledge or they deal with aspects of English such as grammatical structures or idiomatic expressions. There are lots of "Aha! Tips" to help you understand the text.

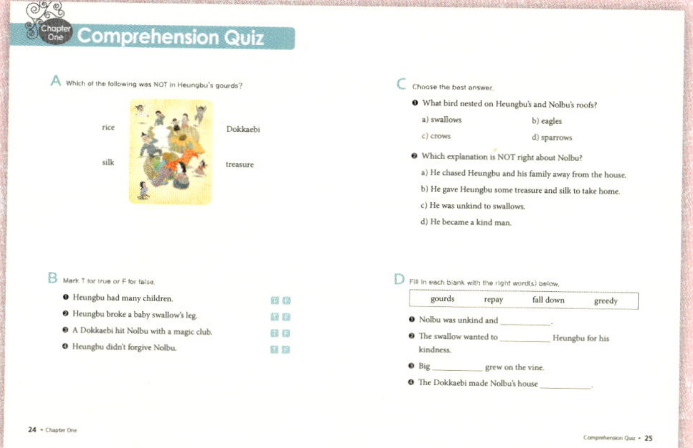

## •Comprehension Quiz

After reading one chapter, solve various questions to find out if you fully understand the content.

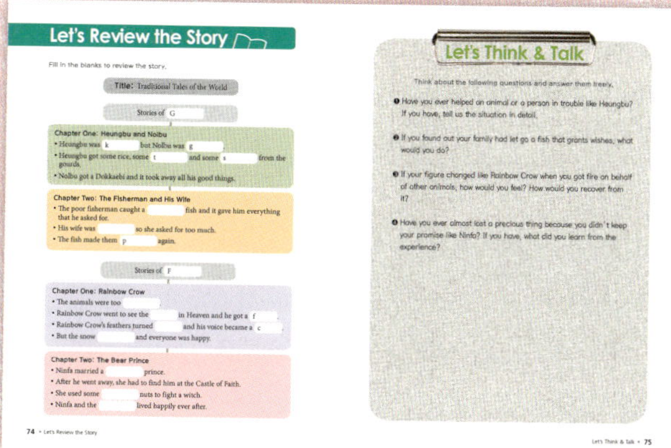

## •Let's Review the Story /
## •Let's Think & Talk

Fill in the blanks in the organizer to summarize the whole story. Express your own thinking and feelings about the story by answering the questions. You can build up logic and reasoning skills for your essay examinations in the future.

## Appendix

### Audio CD

In the CD audio book form, the texts are read vividly by American professional voice actors.
(MP3 files downloaded for free)

### After-reading Test

Solve an additionally provided After-reading Test for each book.

### The Korean translation, Answer Keys, a Word Quiz, a Word List, and Aha! Tips for each book

You can download them for free at *www.ihappyhouse.co.kr* or *www.darakwon.co.kr*

# Before Reading

## Traditional Tales of the World

Level 1–10,
Lexile® 180L

### Traditional tales with fun and lessons

Do you have memories of your grandma telling you traditional bedtime tales? Traditional tales have been passed down from generation to generation since the old days and many of them teach us lessons. Even though the characters, including the animal characters, settings and events in stories are described differently depending on the country the story comes from, the main themes or lessons from the stories are often similar.

In the book, we will read four eastern and western traditional tales dealing with two different themes. There are two traditional tales about 'greed,' one from Korea and one from Germany, and two traditional tales about 'faith,' one is Native American and one is Mexican. The first two show how people will end up if they have endless greed, while the other two show why trusting each other is important and what will happen if that faith is broken. Now let's plunge into the fun of traditional tales.

## Heungbu and Nolbu

Heungbu doesn't have much but his good heart while Nolbu has a lot but he doesn't share with his brother and he wants even more.  What will happen to these brothers?

## The Fisherman and His Wife

The poor fisherman's wife has endless greed. At first, she wants a house. Next, she wants a palace. Later, she wants to be a queen. What will she want next? Will the fish that grants wishes make all her wishes come true?

## Rainbow Crow

In North America, it is told that crows originally had rainbow feathers and beautiful voices. Let's find out the reason why they came to have black feathers and a harsh caw voice as they do now through this story.

## The Bear Prince

Ninfa is married to an enchanted prince who was cursed into being a bear during the day by a witch. Ninfa broke the promise that the Bear Prince asked her to keep because she didn't want her beloved husband to turn into a bear anymore. Will they be able to be happy again?

# Contents

# Traditional Tales of the World


2　About Wise & Wide

4　How to Use This Book

6　Before Reading

**Stories of Greed**
Chapter One

10　Heungbu and Nolbu(Korean Story)

24　Comprehension Quiz

Chapter Two

26　The Fisherman and His Wife(German Story)

40　Comprehension Quiz

**Stories of Faith**
Chapter One

44　Rainbow Crow(Native American Story)

56　Comprehension Quiz

Chapter Two

58　The Bear Prince(Mexican Story)

72　Comprehension Quiz

74　Let's Review the Story

75　Let's Think & Talk

76　Let's Review the Story (Answers)

79　After-reading Test

# Stories of Greed

# Heungbu and Nolbu
## (Korean Story)

Once, there were two brothers.

Their names were Heungbu and Nolbu.

Heungbu was the younger brother.

He was very kind.

Nolbu was the older brother.

He was very unkind.

Nolbu was also greedy.

He wanted everything for himself.

People liked Heungbu.

They did not like Nolbu.

Nolbu was jealous.

He hated Heungbu.

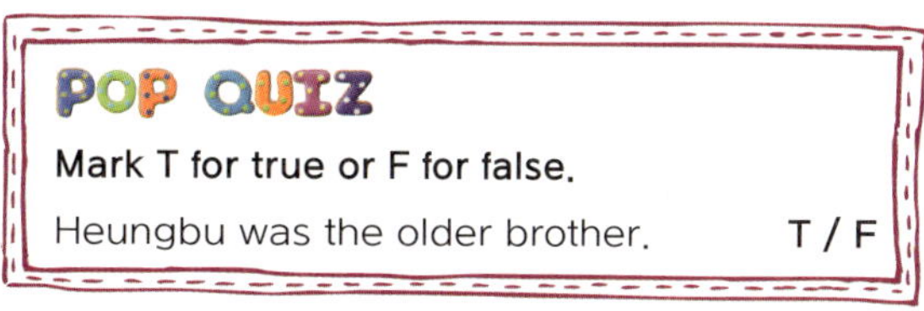


## KEY WORDS

- Korean
- story
- once
- there is[are] ~
- brother
- name
- younger

- kind
- older
- unkind(↔ kind)
- also
- greedy (*cf*. greed)
- want
- everything

- oneself
- people
- like
- jealous
- hate

The two brothers grew up.

Each of them found a wife.

Nolbu had one child.

Heungbu had many children.

Both families lived in the same house.

"Heungbu, your children eat too much!" said
Nolbu.

"We will run out of food.

You must leave this house."

Heungbu and his family left the house.

They were very sad.

They went to live in a small house.

They had no food.

So Heungbu went to visit Nolbu.

"Brother, please give me some food," said Heungbu.

"No," said Nolbu.

He chased Heungbu away.

**KEY WORDS**

- **grow up** (*cf.* grow (grow-grew-grown))
- **each of**
- **find** (find-found-found)
- **wife**
- **child** (*cf.* children)
- **both**
- **family**
- **live**
- **same**
- **eat** (eat-ate-eaten)

- **too**
- **will + *Verb***
- **run out of** (run-ran-run)
- **must + *Verb***
- **leave** (leave-left-left)
- **so**
- **visit**
- **please**
- **give** (give-gave-given)
- **chase ~ away** (*cf.* chase)

Heungbu went to the kitchen.

Nolbu's wife was there.

"Please give me some rice," said Heungbu.

"No," said Nolbu's wife.

She chased Heungbu away.

Heungbu went home.

He was very sad.

"I have no food," he said.

Spring came.

Swallows made a nest under the edge of
Heungbu's roof.

Heungbu was kind to them.

A baby swallow fell out of the nest.

It broke its leg.

Heungbu made its leg better.

The swallow
wanted to repay
Heungbu for his
kindness.
The swallow
gave him a seed.

Heungbu planted the seed.

It grew into a vine.

The vine grew bigger and bigger.

Big gourds grew on the vine.

Heungbu picked three gourds.

He cut them open.

Inside the first gourd was rice.

Inside the second gourd was treasure.

Inside the third gourd was silk.

Heungbu and his family ate some rice.

They gave the rest to hungry people.

They sold some treasure.

They sold some silk.

Heungbu and his family became rich!

**KEY WORDS**

- plant
- vine
- bigger (cf. comparative form + and + comparative form)
- gourd
- pick

- cut (cut-cut-cut)
- inside
- first
- second
- treasure
- third

- silk
- rest
- hungry
- sell (sell-sold-sold)
- become (become-became-become)
- rich

Nolbu came to visit Heungbu. 

"How did this happen?" said Nolbu.

Heungbu told him the story.

Heungbu gave Nolbu some treasure and silk

to take home.

Spring came again.

This time, the swallows made a nest under the edge of Nolbu's roof.

But Nolbu was unkind to them.

He took a baby swallow from the nest.

He broke its leg.

He pretended to make it better.

**POP QUIZ**

**What did Nolbu do to the baby swallow?**

ⓐ He broke its wing.
ⓑ He broke its leg.

### KEY WORDS

- happen
- tell (tell-told-told)
- take (take-took-taken)
- again
- pretend to + *Verb*

The baby swallow gave Nolbu a seed.

Nolbu planted the seed.

It grew into a vine.

Big gourds grew on the vine.

Nolbu picked three gourds.

"I will be rich!" he said.

He cut open the first gourd.

A Dokkaebi jumped out of the gourd.

"You have done bad things!" said the
Dokkaebi.
The Dokkaebi hit Nolbu with a magic club.
The Dokkaebi made Nolbu's house fall down.
The Dokkaebi chased Nolbu's family away.

**KEY WORDS**

- Dokkaebi
- jump out of
- **do bad things** (do-did-done)(*cf.* bad things)
- **hit** (hit-hit-hit)
- with
- **magic club** (*cf.* magic)
- fall down

Nolbu had no house.

He had no food.

He had no family.

He went to visit Heungbu.

"Brother, I am sorry," said Nolbu. 

"Please forgive me."

Heungbu forgave Nolbu.

Nolbu became a kind man.

He lived with Heungbu's family.

They all lived happily for ever after.

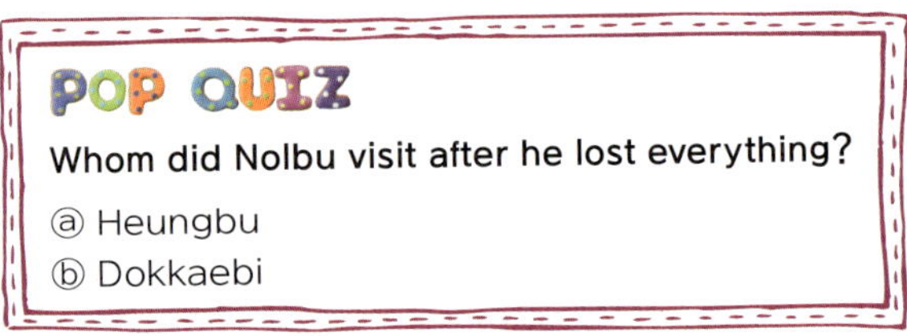


**KEY WORDS**

- sorry
- forgive (forgive-forgave-forgiven)

- happily
- ever after

# Chapter One  Comprehension Quiz

**A**  Which of the following was NOT in Heungbu's gourds?

rice

silk

Dokkaebi

treasure

**B**  Mark T for true or F for false.

❶ Heungbu had many children.  T F

❷ Heungbu broke a baby swallow's leg.  T F

❸ A Dokkaebi hit Nolbu with a magic club.  T F

❹ Heungbu didn't forgive Nolbu.  T F

**C** Choose the best answer.

**❶** What bird nested on Heungbu's and Nolbu's roofs?

    a) swallows                         b) eagles

    c) crows                            d) sparrows

**❷** Which explanation is NOT right about Nolbu?

    a) He chased Heungbu and his family away from the house.

    b) He gave Heungbu some treasure and silk to take home.

    c) He was unkind to swallows.

    d) He became a kind man.

**D** Fill in each blank with the right word(s) below.

| gourds | repay | fall down | greedy |
|---|---|---|---|

**❶** Nolbu was unkind and ______________.

**❷** The swallow wanted to ______________ Heungbu for his kindness.

**❸** Big ______________ grew on the vine.

**❹** The Dokkaebi made Nolbu's house ______________.

# The Fisherman and His Wife
## (German Story)

Once, there was a fisherman.
He lived with his wife.
The fisherman and his wife were very poor.
They lived in a dirty hut.
The hut was by the sea.

**KEY WORDS**

- fisherman
- German
- poor (↔ rich)
- dirty
- hut
- by
- sea

One day, the fisherman went fishing.

He caught a flat fish.

"Please do not eat me," said the fish.

"I am not really a fish.

I am a prince."

The fisherman was kind.

He let the fish go.

**KEY WORDS**

- one day
- go + *Verb*-ing (go-went-gone)
- fish
- catch (catch-caught-caught)

- flat fish (*cf*. flat)
- really
- prince
- let ~ go (let-let-let)

The fisherman went home to tell his wife about it.

"You fool!" said his wife.

"The fish is magical.

Go back and ask it for a house."

So the fisherman went back to the sea.

He called for the fish.

"Oh, flat fish, flat fish, come to me," he called. 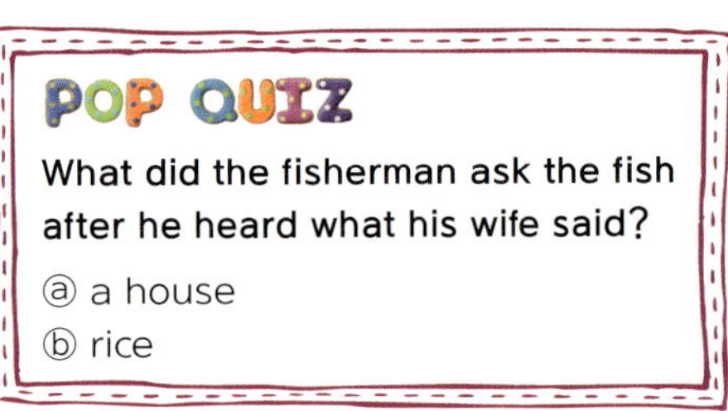

POP QUIZ

What did the fisherman ask the fish after he heard what his wife said?

ⓐ a house
ⓑ rice



**KEY WORDS**

- about
- fool
- magical
- go back

- ask
- call for (*cf.* call)
- come to

The fish came.

"What do you want?" it said.

"My wife wants a house," said the fisherman.

"Go home," said the fish.

"She has a house."

The fisherman went home.

There was his wife.

There was a house!

The fisherman's wife was happy.

After a while, the fisherman's wife was
unhappy. 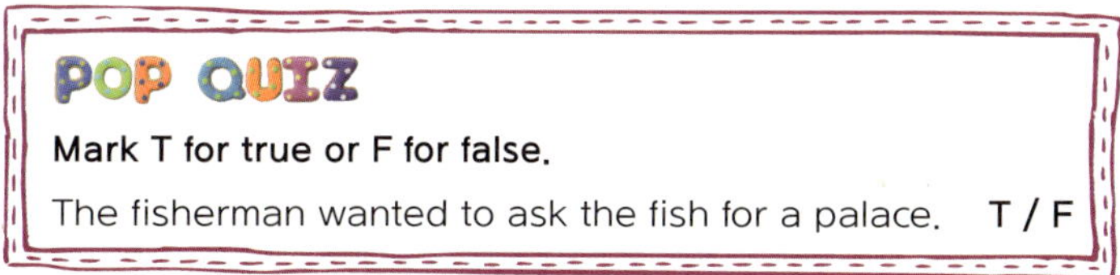

"Go and see the fish," she said.

"Ask it for a palace."

The fisherman did not want to ask for more.

But his wife got angry.

He went back to the sea.

He called for the fish.

"Oh, flat fish, flat fish, come to me," he called.

> ### POP QUIZ
> Mark T for true or F for false.
> The fisherman wanted to ask the fish for a palace.   T / F

**KEY WORDS**

- after a while
- **unhappy** (↔ happy)
- **see** (see-saw-seen)
- **palace**
- **more**
- **get angry** (*cf.* get (get-got-gotten))

The fish came.

"What do you want?" it said.

"My wife wants a palace," said the fisherman.

"Go home," said the fish.

"She has a palace."

The fisherman went home.

There was his wife.

There was a palace!

The fisherman's wife was happy.

After a while, the fisherman's wife was unhappy.

"Go and see the fish," she said.

"I want us to be a king and a queen."

The fisherman did not want to ask for more.

"I do not want to be a king," he said.

But his wife got angry.

"I want to be a queen," she said.

**KEY WORDS**

- king
- queen

The fisherman went back to the sea.

He called for the fish.

"Oh, flat fish, flat fish, come to me," he called.

The fish came.

"What do you want?" it said.

"My wife wants to be a queen," said the fisherman.

"Go home," said the fish.

"She is a queen."

The fisherman went home.

There was his wife.

She was a queen!

The palace was bigger.

Everything was made of gold. Aha!

The fisherman's wife was happy.

After a while, the fisherman's wife was
unhappy.

"What is wrong?" said the fisherman.

"You have everything you wanted."

But his wife was angry.

"I want to be like God," she said.

"I want the sun and the moon to do as I tell
them."

The fisherman was sad that his wife was so
greedy.

But he went back to the sea.

He called for the fish.

"Oh, flat fish, flat fish, come to me," he called.

The fish came.

"What do you want?" it said.

"My wife wants to be like God," said the
fisherman.

"Go home," said the fish.

"She will never be happy.

She is too greedy.

She is sitting by a dirty hut again."

The fisherman went home.

The palace was gone.

His wife sat by a dirty hut.

They lived there for ever after.

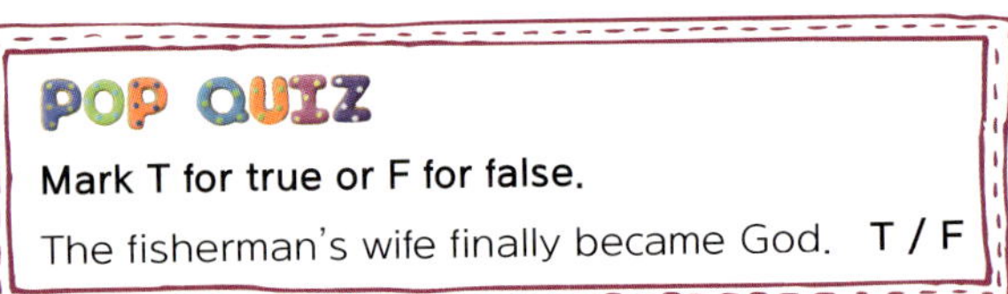

**A** Which of the following did the fisherman's wife NOT want to have or become?

**B** Mark T for true or F for false.

❶ The fisherman and his wife lived in a dirty hut for ever after.    T F

❷ The fisherman caught a flat fish and ate it.    T F

❸ The flat fish was magical.    T F

❹ The flat fish thought the fisherman's wife will never be happy.    T F

 Choose the best answer.

❶ Who really was the fish caught by the fisherman?

    a) a prince             b) a wizard

    c) a fisherman          d) a queen

❷ Which one is NOT right according to the story?

    a) The fisherman called for the fish many times for his wife.

    b) When the fisherman caught a flat fish, he let the fish go.

    c) The fisherman's wife wanted to be the sun and the moon.

    d) Finally the palace was gone.

**D** Fill in each blank with the right word below.

| ask | gold | greedy | poor |
|---|---|---|---|

❶ The fisherman and his wife were very _____________.

❷ The fisherman did not want to _____________ for more to the flat fish.

❸ The fisherman was sad that his wife was so _____________.

❹ The palace was made of _____________.

# Stories of Faith

# Rainbow Crow
## (Native American Story)

One day, when the world was young, snow
began to fall.

The animals liked the snow.

They played in it.

Then, they began to feel cold.

The snow got deeper and deeper.

The animals got colder and colder.

**KEY WORDS**

- crow
- Native American
- world
- young
- animal

- then
- begin (begin-began-begun)
- feel (feel-felt-felt)
- deeper
- colder

"We must do something!" they said.

"We will die."

"I know what to do," said the owl.

"We will send a message to the Creator.

He made us all.

We will ask him to warm the world again."



**KEY WORDS**

- something
- die
- **know** (know-knew-known)
- owl

- **send** (send-sent-sent)
- message
- the Creator
- warm

"Who will go?" asked the animals.

"I will go," said Rainbow Crow. 

He had faith that the Creator would help.

Rainbow Crow had beautiful feathers.

They were all the colors of the rainbow.

Rainbow Crow sang beautiful songs.

His voice was like sweet raindrops.

The Creator lived in Heaven.

It was a long way to go.

Rainbow Crow flew past the trees.

He flew past the clouds.

He flew past the moon and the sun.

He even flew past the stars.

It was a long way.

But the Crow wanted to reach the Creator.

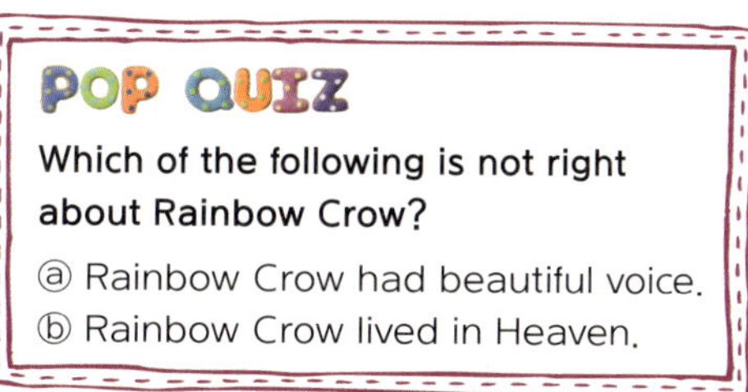



**KEY WORDS**

- faith
- help
- feather
- color
- **sing** (sing-sang-sung)

- song
- voice
- sweet
- raindrop
- Heaven

- way
- **fly** (fly-flew-flown)
- past
- even
- reach

At last, Rainbow Crow reached Heaven.

He began to sing a beautiful song.

"Who is that?" said the Creator.

"I love your beautiful song.

What can I give you?"

"Please stop the snow," said the Rainbow
Crow.

"It is too cold.

We will die.

I have faith that you will help us."

"The ground needs snow," said the Creator.

"You will not die.

I will give you fire.

It will keep you warm."

**KEY WORDS**

- at last
- love
- can + *Verb*
- stop
- ground

- need
- fire
- keep (keep-kept-kept)
- stick
- put (put-put-put)

- burn
- bright
- beak

The Creator took a stick.

He put it into the hot sun.

The stick burned, hot and bright.

"Take this," said the Creator.

"Take it home."

Rainbow Crow took the stick.

He took it in his beak.

He flew home as fast as he could.

The stick burned, hot and bright.

He flew past the sun.

His tail caught fire.

It turned black.

He flew past the moon.

All his feathers caught fire.

They turned black.



- as + *Adjective*/*Adverb* + as + *Subject* + could
- tail
- catch fire
- turn

He flew past the clouds.

Smoke got into his throat.

His voice became a croak.

But Rainbow Crow kept on flying.

His throat hurt.

He was tired.

But he did not give up.

**KEY WORDS**

- smoke
- get into
- throat
- croak

- keep on + *Verb*-ing
- hurt (hurt-hurt-hurt)
- give up

But Rainbow Crow was sad.

"My beautiful feathers are black," he said.

"My beautiful voice has gone.

All I can say is, caw, caw!"

Rainbow Crow took the stick home.

He took fire to the animals.

The animals were warm.

The snow melted.

Everyone was happy.

Rainbow Crow felt some wind on his face.

The Creator spoke through the wind.

When Rainbow Crow took the fire to the animals, what happened?

ⓐ Rainbow Crow's voice became beautiful.
ⓑ The snow melted.

"Do not be sad," said the Creator.

"You will be safe now.

Humans will not hunt you.

Your flesh tastes of smoke.

They will not catch you to eat you.

Your feathers are black.

They will not catch you to look at you.

Your voice is not beautiful.

They will not catch you to listen to you sing.

You will be free."

**KEY WORDS**

- safe
- human
- hunt
- flesh
- taste of
- look at
- listen to
- free
- wise

The Creator was very wise.

"Caw, caw!" said Rainbow Crow. 

"Thank you!"

**Chapter One** # Comprehension Quiz

**A** Which characteristic did Rainbow Crow NOT have before it got fire from the Creator?

black feathers          colors of the rainbow

beautiful voice

**B** Mark T for true or F for false.

❶ Rainbow Crow took the stick in his wings.  T  F

❷ All Rainbow Crow's feathers turned black because of the fire.  T  F

❸ The Creator didn't love Rainbow Crow's beautiful song.  T  F

❹ Rainbow Crow kept on flying to give fire to the animals.  T  F

 Choose the best answer.

**❶** What did Rainbow Crow visit the Creator for?

a) to ask the Creator to warm the world again

b) to sing beautiful songs

c) to make his feathers black

d) to see the clouds

**❷** What is NOT right about the Creator according the story?

a) The Creator lived in Heaven.

b) The Creator helped the animal to stop the snow.

c) The Creator gave water Rainbow Crow to keep the animals warm.

d) The Creator was very wise.

D Fill in each blank with the right word below.

| stick | free | reach | fall |
|---|---|---|---|

**❶** When the world was young, snow began to ________________.

**❷** Rainbow Crow wanted to ______________ the Creator.

**❸** The Creator put a ______________ into the hot sun.

**❹** The Creator said the Crow will be ______________.

# The Bear Prince
## (Mexican Story)

Once, there was a woodcutter.

He was very poor.

He had three beautiful daughters.

The woodcutter went into the forest.

He met a bear.

"I will eat you!" said the bear.

"Please do not eat me," said the woodcutter.

"You may marry my youngest daughter.

She is called Ninfa."

**POP QUIZ**

Whom did the woodcutter allow the bear that he met in the forest to marry?

ⓐ his youngest daughter
ⓑ his sister

Ninfa married the bear.

When night came, he said some magic words.

He turned into a prince!



**KEY WORDS**

- Mexican
- woodcutter
- daughter
- go into
- forest
- **meet** (meet-met-met)

- may + *Verb*
- marry
- youngest
- **magic words** (*cf.* word)
- turn into

When morning came, he said some magic
words.

He turned back into a bear.

"You must not tell my secret," he said.

"A witch put a spell on me."

Ninfa went to visit her family.

Her sisters laughed at her.

"You married a bear!" they said.

Ninfa told them the prince's secret.

## POP QUIZ

How did the prince become a bear
again when morning came?

ⓐ by saying some magic words
ⓑ by putting a gag over his mouth

**KEY WORDS**

- turn back into
- secret
- witch
- put a spell on (*cf.* spell)
- laugh at

- stay
- asleep
- tie ~ up
- put a gag over one's mouth
  (*cf.* gag / over)

"I love him," she said.

"I do not want him to be a bear.

I want him to stay human."

"When he is asleep, tie him up," said one of

her sisters. Aha!

"Put a gag over his mouth.

Then he will not turn back into a bear."

That night, Ninfa tied up the prince.

"I'm sorry.

My sisters told me to do this."

She put a gag over his mouth.

In the morning, he woke up.

He could not say the magic words.

He stayed a prince!

Ninfa was happy.

But the prince was sad.

**KEY WORDS**

- **wake up** (wake-woke-woken)
- **could**
- **look for**
- **castle**
- **vanish**

"You broke your promise," he said.

"You told my secret.

Now I must go.

Look for the Castle of Faith.

You will find me there."

The prince vanished.

Ninfa was very sad.

She set out to look for the Castle of Faith.

She came to a forest.

A wizard lived there.

"Where is the Castle of Faith?" asked Ninfa.

"I do not know," said the wizard.

He gave her three magic nuts.

"If you are in trouble, break open the nuts,"
he said.

Ninfa walked on.

She came to a house.

She knocked on the door.

A woman opened the door.

"Who lives here?" asked Ninfa.

"The Sun lives here," said the woman.

"He will burn you if he finds you!"

Just then, the Sun came in.

He filled the house with light and heat.

"Please help me!" shouted Ninfa.

"I need to find the Castle of Faith."

"It is a long way from here," said the Sun.

"My friend, the Wind, will take you.

He lives along the path."

Ninfa walked on.

She came to another house.

The Wind lived there.

She knocked on the door.

"What do you want?" screamed the Wind.

"Will you take me to the Castle of Faith?"
asked Ninfa.

"Yes, I will," said the Wind.

Ninfa flew on the back of the Wind.

They flew to the Castle of Faith.

There was a party going on.

Ninfa knocked on the door.

A servant opened the door.

"I would like to see the prince," said Ninfa. 

"Today is his wedding day," said the servant.

"He is dancing with his new princess."

Ninfa was very sad.

She went into the castle.

She saw the prince and the new princess.

<br>

## POP QUIZ

**What day was the day when Ninfa arrived at the Castle of the Faith?**

ⓐ the prince's wedding day
ⓑ the prince's birthday

**KEY WORDS**

- another
- scream
- back
- party
- go on
- servant

- would like to + *Verb*
- wedding day (*cf.* wedding)
- dance
- new
- princess

The new princess was really an evil witch.

She tricked the prince into marrying her.

The prince saw Ninfa.

"There is my love!" he called.

"Bring her to me."

But the music was too loud.

The servants did not hear him.

"Get her out of here!" screamed the witch.

Ninfa broke open the first magic nut.

She turned into a rat.

The witch turned into a cat.

The witch chased Ninfa.

Ninfa jumped onto the prince's plate.

**KEY WORDS**

- evil
- **trick ... into ~** (*cf.* trick)
- **bring** (bring-brought-brought)
- **loud**
- **hear** (hear-heard-heard)

- **get ... out of ~**
- **rat**
- **jump onto**
- **plate**

Ninfa broke open the second magic nut.

She turned into a grain of rice. **Aha!**

She hid in the rice on the prince's plate.

The witch turned into a chicken.

She began to eat the rice.

Ninfa broke open the third magic nut.

She turned into a wolf.

The wolf ate the chicken.

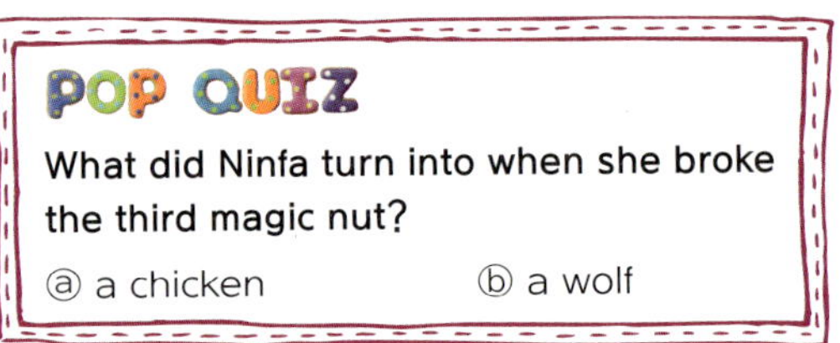



**KEY WORDS**

- **a grain of rice** (*cf.* grain)
- **hide** (hide-hid-hidden)

- **chicken**
- **dead** (↔ alive)

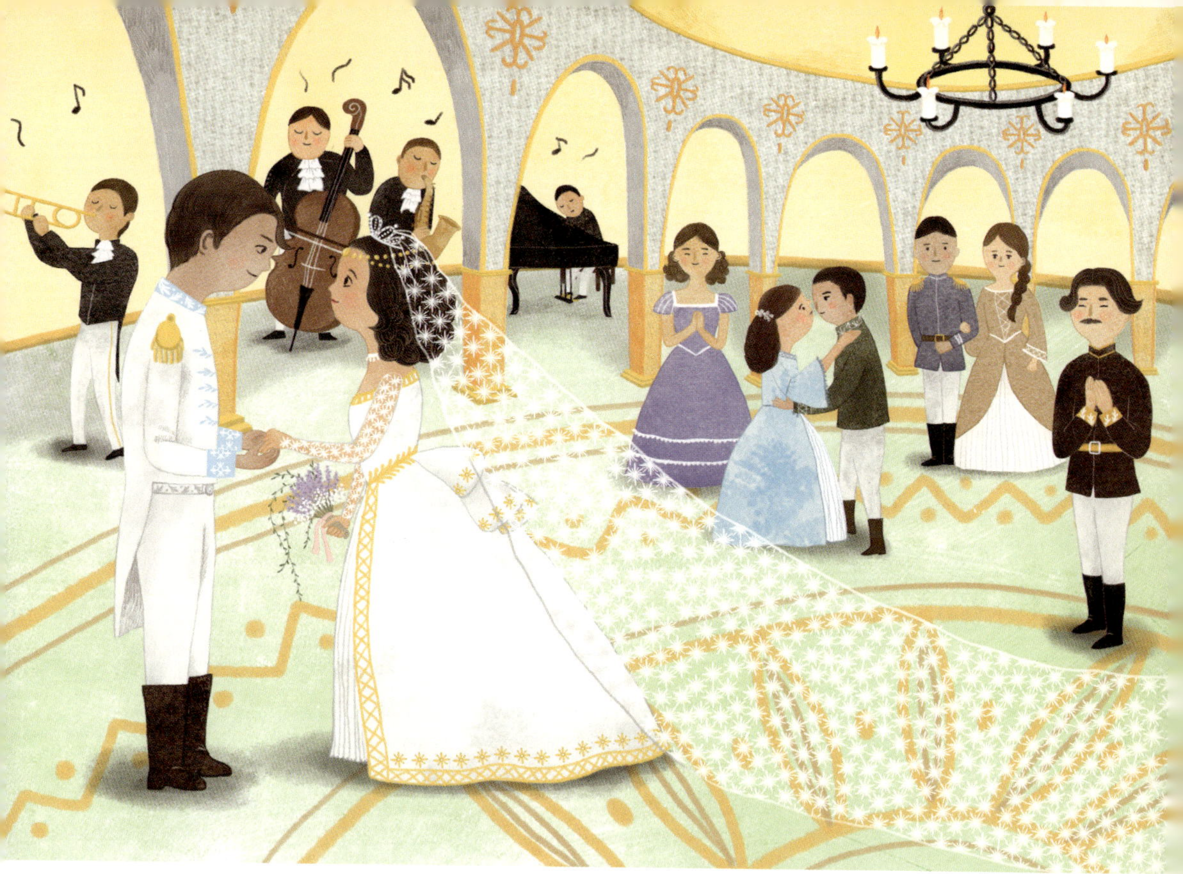

The witch was dead!

Ninfa turned back into a human.

She married the prince.

They lived happily ever after.

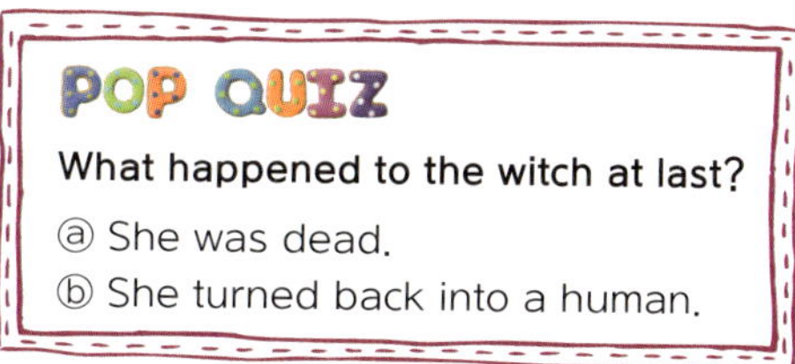

**A** Mark T for true or F for false

**❶** The woodcutter had four beautiful daughters.　T　F

**❷** The bear that Ninfa married turned into a prince at night.　T　F

**❸** The bear prince said Ninfa must not tell his secret.　T　F

**❹** Ninfa wanted the bear prince to be a bear.　T　F

**B** Fill in each blank with the right word(s) below.

| took | youngest | magic | set out |
| --- | --- | --- | --- |

**❶** The bear prince married the woodcutter's _____________ daughter.

**❷** After the bear said some _____________ words, it turned into a prince!

**❸** Ninfa _____________ to look for the Castle of Faith.

**❹** The Wind _____________ Ninfa to the Castle of Faith.

**C** Choose the best answer.

**❶** What did NOT Ninfa turn into through magic nuts?

a) a wolf

b) a rat

c) a grain of rice

d) a cat

**❷** Why did the prince have to turn into a bear during the day?

a) because a witch put a spell on him

b) because he wanted to stay a bear

c) because he didn't get three magic nuts from a wizard

d) because Ninfa put a gag over his mouth

**❸** Whom did Ninfa NOT meet on her way to the Castle of the Faith?

a) a wizard

b) the Sun

c) the Wind

d) her father

# Let's Review the Story

Fill in the blanks to review the story.

**Title:** Traditional Tales of the World

Stories of  G

## Chapter One: Heungbu and Nolbu
- Heungbu was  k          but Nolbu was  g          .
- Heungbu got some rice, some  t          and some  s          from the gourds.
- Nolbu got a Dokkaebi and it took away all his good things.

## Chapter Two: The Fisherman and His Wife
- The poor fisherman caught a            fish and it gave him everything that he asked for.
- His wife was            so she asked for too much.
- The fish made them  p          again.

Stories of  F

## Chapter One: Rainbow Crow
- The animals were too            .
- Rainbow Crow went to see the            in Heaven and he got a  f      .
- Rainbow Crow's feathers turned            and his voice became a  c      .
- But the snow            and everyone was happy.

## Chapter Two: The Bear Prince
- Ninfa married a            prince.
- After he went away, she had to find him at the Castle of Faith.
- She used some            nuts to fight a witch.
- Ninfa and the            lived happily ever after.

# Let's Think & Talk

**Think about the following questions and answer them freely.**

❶ Have you ever helped an animal or a person in trouble like Heungbu? If you have, tell us the situation in detail.

❷ If you found out your family had let go a fish that grants wishes, what would you do?

❸ If your figure changed like Rainbow Crow when you got fire on behalf of other animals, how would you feel? How would you recover from it?

❹ Have you ever almost lost a precious thing because you didn't keep your promise like Ninfa? If you have, what did you learn from the experience?

# Let's Review the Story

**Title:** Traditional Tales of the World

Stories of  Greed

**Chapter One: Heungbu and Nolbu**
- Heungbu was  kind  but Nolbu was  greedy .
- Heungbu got some rice, some  treasure  and some  silk  from the gourds.
- Nolbu got a Dokkaebi and it took away all his good things.

**Chapter Two: The Fisherman and His Wife**
- The poor fisherman caught a  flat  fish and it gave him everything that he asked for.
- His wife was  greedy  so she asked for too much.
- The fish made them  poor  again.

Stories of  Faith

**Chapter One: Rainbow Crow**
- The animals were too  cold .
- Rainbow Crow went to see the Creator in Heaven and he got a  fire .
- Rainbow Crow's feathers turned  black  and his voice became a  croak .
- But the snow  melted  and everyone was happy.

**Chapter Two: The Bear Prince**
- Ninfa married a  bear  prince.
- After he went away, she had to find him at the Castle of Faith.
- She used some  magic  nuts to fight a witch.
- Ninfa and the  prince  lived happily ever after.

# After-reading Test

- Traditional Tales of the World
- Level 1
- 18 Questions

  (Vocabulary 4 / Reading Comprehension 10 /

  Sentence Structure & Grammar 4)

1. Which of the following word does NOT indicate people's mood or feeling?
   ① happy
   ② angry
   ③ magical
   ④ jealous

2. Which of the following is NOT a pair of opposites?
   ① kind ↔ unkind
   ② fool ↔ wise
   ③ love ↔ hate
   ④ set out ↔ vanish

3. Which pair has the wrong past tense form of the listed verb?
   ① find − found
   ② grow − grew
   ③ catch − caught
   ④ sit − sit

4. Choose the right word for the blank.

   Everything was __________ of gold.

   ① liked
   ② fell
   ③ felt
   ④ made

5. What did Heungbu do to the baby swallow?
   ① He built a nest for it.
   ② He gave it some food.
   ③ He helped it to fly.
   ④ He made its leg better.

6. What did the Dokkaebi coming from Nolbu's gourd NOT do?
   ① It hit Nolbu with a magic club.
   ② It made Nolbu's house fall down.
   ③ It chased Nolbu's family away.
   ④ It made Nolbu ill.

7. What did the fisherman's wife NOT want?
   ① to live in a palace
   ② to be a queen
   ③ to be like God
   ④ to have a baby

8. How did the fisherman's wife feel at first when she got a house thanks to the
   fish's magic?
   ① angry                     ② happy
   ③ afraid                    ④ sad

9.  Why did the fisherman become sad?

   ① because his wife was so greedy

   ② because he wanted to eat the fish

   ③ because the fish was gone

   ④ because he lost the palace


10. What characteristic is right about Rainbow Crow?

   ① He liked to fly over rainbows.

   ② He was able to make rainbows.

   ③ His feathers were all the colors of the rainbow.

   ④ He was made out of a rainbow.


11. Why did Rainbow Crow become sad after it brought fire to animals?

   ① None of the animals thanked him.

   ② He missed playing in the snow.

   ③ He wanted to live in Heaven.

   ④ He lost his beautiful voice and feathers.


12. Why was the Bear Prince sad when he couldn't turn into a bear?

   ① He liked being a bear.

   ② Ninfa broke the promise and he had to go.

   ③ He was afraid that the witch would be angry.

   ④ He thought that Ninfa would not love him anymore.

13. What did the witch turn into when Ninfa turned into a rat?
　① a horse
　② a dog
　③ a cat
　④ a dragon

14. How did the witch die?
　① The prince killed her with a sword.
　② The Sun came and burned her up.
　③ The Wind blew her over a cliff.
　④ Ninfa turned into a wolf and ate her.

※ Choose the wrong part of the sentence. (15~17)

15.
You must leaving this house.
　①　　②　　③　　　④

16.
Nolbu came visiting Heungbu.
　①　　②　　③　　　④

17.



18. Choose the correct word for the blank.

I would like to ___________ the prince.

① seeing                    ② seen
③ saw                       ④ see

# Memo

# Memo 

**Sarah J. Dodd**

Sarah J. Dodd is an experienced primary school teacher who resides in the UK, but has also lived and taught in Australia. She has a PhD in Science and a certificate in Creative Writing. She has published several books for children: "An Angel Anyway" (Anyway Press, 2008) the "Little Angels" series (Lion Children's Books, 2009/10), "The Lion Picture Bible" (Lion Children's Books, 2015) and "Legs: the tale of a meerkat lost and found" (Lion Children's Books, 2015). Her poetry for children has also been highly commended and published in the anthology "Let in the Stars" (Manchester Metropolitan University, 2014).

She is currently working on further picture books for the very young, and a novel for older children.

# Traditional Tales of the World

Retold by Sarah J. Dodd
Illustrated by Satbyeol Son

First Published in October 2017

Editorial Manager: Juyon Choi
Editors: Jiyeong Park, Kyunghee Jang
Designers: Eunhee Lee, Elim
Cover Designer: Eunhee Lee

Published and distributed by

Darakwon Bldg., 64-1 Jandari-ro, Mapo-gu, Seoul, Korea 04031
Tel: 82-2-736-2031(ext. 250)     Fax: 82-2-732-2037
Homepage: www.ihappyhouse.co.kr
Publisher: Kyudo Chung



ISBN: 978-89-6653-549-1 18740 / 978-89-6653-156-1 18740(set)

[Components]
• 1 Audio CD (Recording Studio: Aram)
• Answer Keys & Korean Translation: Free download at www.ihappyhouse.co.kr